Harry Potter™

RON WEASLEY™

Cinematic Guide

SCHOLASTIC LTD.

www.harrypotter.com

Scholastic Children's Books
Euston House, 24 Eversholt Street,
London NW1 1DB, UK

A division of Scholastic Ltd
London ~ New York ~ Toronto ~ Sydney ~ Auckland
Mexico City ~ New Delhi ~ Hong Kong

First published in the US by Scholastic Inc, 2016
Published in the UK by Scholastic Ltd, 2016

By Felicity Baker
Art Direction: Rick DeMonico
Page Design: Two Red Shoes Design

ISBN 978 1407 17317 7

Printed and bound in Germany

2 4 6 8 10 9 7 5 3 1

Papers used by Scholastic Children's Books are made from
wood grown in sustainable forests.

www.scholastic.co.uk

Contents

Film Beginnings

Upon their first meeting,
Ron Weasley quickly becomes best
friends with Harry Potter. For Ron,
attendance at Hogwarts is expected:
the Weasleys are a large wizarding
family, with Ron the sixth of seven
children. Ron's biggest challenge is
discovering his own path at school
when his many siblings have
been there before him.

Ron's adventure begins when he arrives at Platform Nine and Three-Quarters in King's Cross station to board the Hogwarts Express for the first time.

> *"Now all you've got to do is walk straight at the wall between platforms nine and ten."*
>
> – MOLLY WEASLEY, *HARRY POTTER AND THE PHILOSOPHER'S STONE* FILM

Ron's mother and younger sister Ginny come to the train station to see Ron off to Hogwarts.

On-board, Ron discovers he's in the same compartment as the famous Harry Potter!

The boys get along right away – and
Harry seals the friendship with sweets
he buys from the food trolley.

> "There's chocolate and peppermint. And there's also spinach, liver and tripe."

> – RON WEASLEY, ON BERTIE BOTT'S EVERY FLAVOUR BEANS, *HARRY POTTER AND THE PHILOSOPHER'S STONE* FILM

Ron also meets Hermione Granger, another first year, and initially thinks that she's a know-it-all. It's hard to imagine from this first moment that these three young wizards would become best friends!

Life at Hogwarts

Ron fits right in at Hogwarts. Not only does he become close with Harry and Hermione and other Gryffindor students, but he becomes an important part of Harry's adventures.

After arriving at Hogwarts, Ron is sorted into Gryffindor house – just like his older brothers.

"Ha! Another Weasley. I know just what to do with you – Gryffindor!"

– THE SORTING HAT, *HARRY POTTER AND THE PHILOSOPHER'S STONE* FILM

Ron's new friends, Harry
and Hermione, are sorted
into Gryffindor, too.

Ron and Harry have all their classes together.

Ron and Harry arrive late to their first Transfiguration class with Professor McGonagall.

Ron also has classes with Hermione – much to his dismay, Hermione often tells him what to do.

Ron and his classmates have their first flying lesson with
Madam Hooch.

Not all classes are as thrilling as learning to fly. Ron and Harry
struggle to pay attention in Professor Trelawney's Divination class.

Earmuffs are needed in Herbology class! Ron unearths a young screaming Mandrake whose cries are damaging, if not quite fatal.

Ron faces his greatest fear during Defence Against the Dark Arts class – a giant spider.

Ron and Hermione encourage Harry to teach their fellow students how to defend themselves against the Dark Arts and start Dumbledore's Army.

The trio creates the secret group to teach defensive magical skills to protect them from Lord Voldemort and other Dark forces.

Life at Hogwarts is not just about classes –
there's time for some fun, too.

A trip to Hogsmeade.

Playing wizard chess with Harry.

The Yule Ball, a dance held during the Triwizard Tournament, brings exciting new challenges to Ron and Harry.

Ron and Harry try to work up the courage to ask the beautiful Beauxbatons students to the Yule Ball.

"Mum's sent me a dress."

– RON WEASLEY, *HARRY POTTER AND THE GOBLET OF FIRE* FILM

Ron and Harry attend the Yule Ball with the Patil sisters, Padma and Parvati.

Surprising many, including Ron and Harry, Hermione attends with Viktor Krum, a famous Quidditch player from Durmstrang.

The Weasleys are not only an old wizarding family, but are also a very close and generous clan. Over the course of the films, the Weasleys become a second family to Harry. Like Harry, Ron also makes close friends – and a few enemies – at Hogwarts.

Family, Friends
and Foes

The Weasleys live in a magical home
called The Burrow.

"It's not much, but it's home."

– RON WEASLEY, *HARRY POTTER AND
THE CHAMBER OF SECRETS* FILM

Ron's mum and dad, Arthur and Molly Weasley.

There are many Weasleys, and the family has a special clock to keep track of everyone's whereabouts.

Two of Ron's older brothers, Fred and George, are twins. They are notorious at Hogwarts for making mischief.

Fred and George Weasley take an Ageing Potion to make themselves old enough to enter the Triwizard Tournament. This time, their wizardry backfires!

The Weasley twins' fireworks dragon chases Professor Umbridge, one of their least favourite teachers, right out of the Great Hall!

Ron's younger sister, Ginny,
is a powerful witch.

Ginny proves to be a helpful ally in the fight against Lord Voldemort.

Ginny takes a
special interest
in Harry,
much to Ron's
disapproval.

In addition to the twins, Ron has three more older brothers: Bill, Charlie and Percy.

Bill graduated from Hogwarts before Ron arrived.

Percy, Ron's third-oldest brother, is a prefect at Hogwarts. Unlike Ron, Percy loves having authority and enforcing the rules.

Ron invites his closest friends, Harry and Hermione, to go to the Quidditch World Cup with his family. Their fun is interrupted by Death Eaters.

"As Minister for Magic, it gives me great pleasure to welcome each and every one of you to the final of the four hundred and twenty-second Quidditch World Cup. Let the match begin!"

– CORNELIUS FUDGE, HARRY POTTER AND THE GOBLET OF FIRE FILM

In his sixth year, Ron begins dating
fellow Gryffindor Lavender Brown.

Hermione has feelings for Ron and is devastated about
Ron's relationship with Lavender.

After Ron drinks poison meant for Professor Dumbledore,
Hermione is the first to be by Ron's side – much to Lavender's
dismay. Ron calls out for Hermione in his sleep, revealing that
he may have strong feelings for her.

Even though Ron is a loyal friend and fun to be around, he does have foes.

The most notorious of them are Draco Malfoy and his cohorts, Crabbe and Goyle.

"Red hair and a hand-me-down robe? You must be a Weasley."

– Draco Malfoy, Harry Potter
and the Philosopher's Stone film

> *"Were you in Slytherin and your fate rested with me, the both of you would be on the train home tonight."*
>
> – Professor Snape, *Harry Potter and the Chamber of Secrets* film

Professor Snape appears to dislike Ron almost as much as he dislikes Harry, and he threatens to expel them both from Hogwarts more than once.

Magical Mishaps

From the very beginning, Ron has his ups and downs learning to perform magic. His adventures in the wizarding world often turn quickly into *misadventures*.

After Harry and Ron miss the train to Hogwarts at the start of their second year, the boys find a way to get to school: Mr Weasley's flying car!

"Ron. I should tell you. Most Muggles aren't accustomed to seeing a flying car."

– HARRY POTTER, *HARRY POTTER AND THE CHAMBER OF SECRETS* FILM

The flying car, with Ron and Harry inside, crash-lands into the Whomping Willow on the grounds at Hogwarts.

Mrs Weasley sends Ron a Howler – an angry letter that scolds him in front of the whole school.

"RONALD WEASLEY! How dare you steal that car? I am absolutely disgusted!"

– MRS WEASLEY'S HOWLER, *HARRY POTTER AND THE CHAMBER OF SECRETS* FILM

Sometimes Ron's magical mishaps range from the disgusting to the ridiculous.

Ron's wand breaks after the car crashes. He tries to fix it, but it never quite works the same way.

After Draco insults Hermione, Ron tries to curse him. But the spell goes wrong, and Ron ends up vomiting slugs.

Ron accidentally eats chocolates laced with a love potion that was meant for Harry. As a result, Ron becomes hopelessly lovesick for Romilda Vane.

Ron: "It's no joke! I'm in love with her!"

Harry: "Alright, fine, you're in love with her! Have you ever actually met her?"

– HARRY POTTER AND THE HALF-BLOOD PRINCE FILM

Quidditch

In his sixth year, Ron tries out for the Gryffindor Quidditch team and earns the coveted position of Keeper.

Ron in his Keeper's uniform and gear.

During Quidditch tryouts, Ron makes
some daring saves at the goalpost.

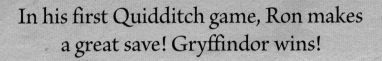

In his first Quidditch game, Ron makes
a great save! Gryffindor wins!

The Quidditch crowd goes wild for Ron!

Post-game celebration for Ron in the Gryffindor common room.

Fighting Dark Forces

Ron is almost always at Harry's side when he encounters Dark forces. He bravely overcomes his fears, and often comes up with resourceful ideas to save the day.

In the first film, Ron, Harry and Hermione search Hogwarts for the Philosopher's Stone. Ron plays a dangerous game of wizard chess in order to help Harry reach the legendary stone.

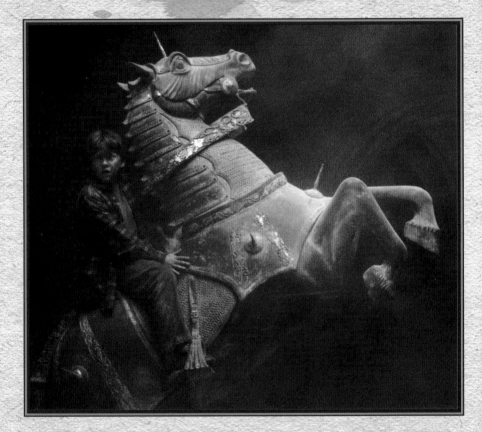

"You understand, right, Harry? Once I make my move, the queen will take me. Then you're free to check the king."

– RON WEASLEY, *HARRY POTTER AND THE PHILOSOPHER'S STONE* FILM

In his third year, Ron learns the scary truth about Scabbers, his pet rat – he's not really a rat at all!

Scabbers turns out to be Peter Pettigrew, one of Lord Voldemort's Death Eaters, in disguise!

Since Ron's parents are in the Order of the Phoenix, a group dedicated to stopping Voldemort, the whole Weasley family – and those associated with them – are in constant danger.

Nagini, Voldemort's snake, attacks Arthur Weasley.

Death Eaters attack The Burrow.

Harry, Ron and Hermione go on their most dangerous mission yet – the hunt for Horcruxes.

Voldemort has concealed parts of his soul in these bewitched objects and creatures. If the trio destroys the Horcruxes, they can then destroy Voldemort. Ron, Harry and Hermione plan to steal a Horcrux during a raid on the Ministry of Magic.

At the Ministry, Dolores Umbridge has a locket that is one of Voldemort's Horcruxes.

Ron, Harry and Hermione steal the locket, but its evil is so powerful that it drives Ron mad enough to abandon his friends.

Ron gets out from under the influence of the Horcrux locket and returns to help his friends.

He saves Harry from drowning in a lake and then uses the Sword of Gryffindor to destroy the locket.

Hermione is furious at Ron for leaving her and Harry at a desperate time.

Ron: "How long do you reckon she'll stay mad at me?"

Harry: "Just keep talking 'bout that little ball of light touching your heart – she'll come 'round."

– HARRY POTTER AND THE DEATHLY HALLOWS – PART 1 FILM

On their hunt for Horcruxes, Snatchers kidnap Ron, Harry and Hermione and bring them to Malfoy Manor, Draco's family home.

Ron uses his Deluminator, a gift from Dumbledore, to turn off the lights so he and Harry can ambush the Death Eaters.

Ron and Harry rescue Hermione from being tortured by Bellatrix Lestrange and escape with Luna Lovegood, Ollivander the wandmaker and the Goblin Griphook.

During the final battle against
Voldemort at Hogwarts, Ron and Hermione
become closer than ever.

After Ron and Hermione destroy another Horcrux, they embrace, admitting their feelings for each other at last.

Ron: "Do you think we'll ever have a quiet year at Hogwarts?"

Harry & Hermione: "No."

Ron: "Yeah, didn't think so. Oh well, what's life without a few dragons?"

– HARRY POTTER AND THE GOBLET OF FIRE FILM